DAD'S RULES FOR MONEY

The Financial Independence Formula

JACK WARREN

Writersgram
Publications

Dad's Rules for Money: The Financial Independence Formula
by Jack Warren

First Impression: September 2024

ISBN: 978-93-5485-847-5
Published by: Writersgram Publications, New Delhi
www.writersgram.com
publications@writersgram.com

Published in India

Jack Warren asserts the moral right to be identified as the author of this book.

I wasn't born into wealth or privilege, nor did I have all the answers when I started out in life. I was just an ordinary guy doing what everyone else seemed to be doing—trying to figure things out as I went. Growing up in a typical middle-class household, I learned the usual lessons: work hard, get a decent job, pay your bills, and hopefully, life will fall into place. For a long time, that's what I did. I worked the 9-to-5 grind, kept up with the bills, and occasionally splurged on weekends to give myself something to look forward to.

But the truth was, I always felt like I was just treading water, never quite getting ahead. I was stressed, often tired, and stuck in a cycle that left me wondering, "Is this it? Is this all there is to life?" Like so many others, I struggled to balance work, personal relationships, and my own mental and physical well-being. I'd spend hours worrying about my finances, how I was going to pay off debt, or why I never seemed to have time for myself. I wasn't living—I was surviving.

Everything changed the day I decided to stop just surviving and start living intentionally. I began taking a hard look at every area of my life—my finances, my health, my relationships, and even the way I spent my time. I realized that if I kept doing what I had always done, I would stay exactly where I was: stuck. So, I started making small changes.

I devoured books on personal finance, time management, and personal development. I started applying what I learned, not just in my bank account, but in my everyday life. I simplified my spending and started saving intentionally. I learned how to manage my time better, prioritize my mental health, and invest in my relationships. It wasn't an overnight transformation—it took years of trial and error, but I began to see real change. I realized that the key wasn't about finding quick fixes; it was about being intentional and disciplined in every area of life.

Eventually, those small changes added up, and I found myself in a place I'd never imagined—free. Free from the financial stress that had weighed me down for so long. Free to spend my time how I wanted. Free to focus on the things that really mattered to me: my health, my relationships, and my personal growth.

Now, I live a simpler, quieter life in the mountains, far removed from the hustle and chaos of city living. Here, I've found the clarity and peace I had been searching for. I'm not isolated because I'm running away from the world; I'm here because I've learned to live life on my terms.

These days, my mission is to help others make the same transformation. I want to show people that you don't have to be rich or privileged to turn your life around. Whether you're stuck in debt, struggling with time management, or feeling overwhelmed by life's daily grind, change is possible. I write not because I have all the answers, but because I've been there—I know what it's like to feel stuck. Through my books, I share what I've learned, hoping that my story can inspire others to take control of their lives and make the changes they've been dreaming of.

Life isn't perfect, and neither am I, but one thing is certain: I've found freedom, and now I'm here to help you find yours.

Jack Warren

INTRODUCTION: DAD'S RULES FOR FINANCIAL FREEDOM

If there's one thing my dad always said, it was this: *"Money is a tool. It can't buy you happiness, but it can give you choices."* Those choices—where to live, how to spend your time, and whom to spend it with—form the foundation of a life lived on your own terms. Growing up, I didn't fully understand the depth of this wisdom. But as I've navigated my own path to financial independence, I've come to realize that Dad's words weren't just advice; they were a formula, a guide to breaking free from the financial constraints that hold so many people back.

This book is about those lessons. It's not about get-rich-quick schemes, or risky investments with the hope of overnight success. It's about the timeless principles my dad lived by—rules that shaped his life and, in turn, shaped mine. These rules helped him, a regular man with a modest income, build security and freedom for our family. And they've helped me to not only maintain that stability but also to grow it, in a way that aligns with my own dreams and values.

I won't pretend that the journey to financial independence was without its challenges. There were times when I questioned the wisdom in Dad's rules. Why save so much when I could be enjoying life now? Why invest in things I didn't fully understand yet? Why avoid debt when it seemed like everyone else was living beyond their means and getting by just fine? But over time, I learned that Dad's rules weren't just about money—they were about building a mindset and a lifestyle that made financial freedom possible, sustainable, and even enjoyable.

The Journey of Generations

Dad's lessons didn't come from textbooks, finance seminars, or corporate boardrooms. They came from his father, my grandpa, a man who knew what it meant to work hard for every dollar. Grandpa never had much, but he had enough. He taught Dad that wealth wasn't just what you earned—it was what you kept, and how you used it. That idea was passed down, not in the form of complex financial jargon, but in simple, actionable rules that shaped our family's approach to money for generations.

Dad built on those lessons. He wasn't a wealthy entrepreneur or a high-powered executive. He worked a regular job, provided for our family, and made sure we never lacked what we needed. But through the principles he lived by, Dad taught me that financial independence isn't just for the rich or the lucky—it's for anyone willing to follow a few key rules consistently over time.

What sets this book apart is the personal journey behind it. These are not just generic principles; they are the actual strategies passed down through my family. Each rule has been tested, refined, and lived by. They've survived economic downturns, personal setbacks, and unexpected challenges. And they aren't meant to be followed in isolation—they're interconnected, forming a cohesive blueprint for financial freedom.

Building Wealth Across Generations

One of the key differences in this book is our focus on creating wealth that lasts beyond one lifetime. My dad didn't just think about his own financial security—he thought about what he could pass down to me and, eventually, to my own children. This generational mindset is what truly sets **Dad's Rules for Money** apart. It's about building a legacy, not just a bank account balance. My dad always said, *"If you're only thinking about yourself, you're thinking too small."*

In a world obsessed with immediate gratification, this long-term view can seem like an outdated way of thinking. But it's the cornerstone of financial independence. Wealth isn't about flashy cars, big houses, or showing off on social media. True wealth is quiet—it's the confidence that comes from knowing you're secure, no matter what happens tomorrow. It's the freedom to make choices based on your values, not your paycheck. And most importantly, it's the ability to pass that security on to the next generation.

What You'll Learn in This Book

The rules my dad followed are simple, but they're not easy. They require discipline, patience, and a willingness to think beyond the moment. But they work. In this book, we'll go through each of these rules in detail—rules that helped my dad achieve financial security and have helped me go even further, towards complete financial independence.

Here's a preview of what we'll cover:

- ✓ **The True Purpose of Money**: Why money is a tool for freedom, not the end goal.

- ✓ **Building Your Financial Foundation**: How saving and investing in yourself first is key to long-term wealth.

- ✓ **Assets vs. Liabilities**: Why understanding the difference can transform your financial outlook.

- ✓ **The Power of Frugality**: How living below your means can set you free, without sacrificing quality of life.

- ✓ **Debt: When and How to Use It**: How smart debt can accelerate your wealth, and why most people get it wrong.

✓ **Legacy Building**: How to create wealth that lasts, and the importance of teaching the next generation.

Each chapter will not only share Dad's practical advice but also real-life examples from our family's journey. I'll show you how I applied these rules—sometimes imperfectly—and what I learned along the way. You'll also find exercises and tips at the end of each chapter to help you start putting these principles into action right away.

A Financial Independence for All

I've written this book for anyone who wants to achieve financial independence, whether you're just starting out or you've been working for years and feel stuck in the *"rat race."* Dad didn't have a fancy degree or a high-paying job, and you don't need one either. What you need is a clear set of rules, a willingness to follow them, and the patience to let time do its work. This isn't about getting rich quickly—it's about getting free steadily.

Financial independence isn't out of reach, no matter where you are in life. With Dad's rules, it's not just possible—it's inevitable. All it takes is the courage to start.

Chapter 1

Rule 1: Understand Money and Its True Purpose

Growing up, I believed money was the ultimate goal. It was the answer to all my questions, the solution to every problem. If we had enough money, life would be better—easier. But as my dad often reminded me, *"Money isn't the end, it's the means."* It took me years to truly grasp what he meant by that, but once I did, everything changed.

You see, most people chase money because they think it will give them security or happiness. They imagine that with enough money, they can finally live the life they've always dreamed of. But the problem with that mindset is that money is not inherently good or bad—it's neutral. It's a tool, like a hammer or a saw, and just like any tool, its value depends entirely on how you use it.

Money as a Tool, Not a Goal

Dad wasn't a millionaire, but he was one of the wisest men I knew. He understood that chasing money for its own sake would only lead to frustration. He often said, *"The real purpose of money is to give you choices. If you treat money like a destination, you'll never get anywhere. But if you see it as a tool, you can build whatever kind of life you want."*

That was a major shift in thinking for me. The difference between those who are constantly stressed about money and those who seem at ease isn't necessarily how much they have—it's how they think about it. When you stop seeing money as the finish line and start seeing it as something that empowers you to make choices, you begin to unlock its true potential.

The truth is, if you don't know what you're working toward—beyond simply accumulating more money—you'll find yourself stuck in a cycle of never having enough. Dad taught me that wealth wasn't about flashy cars or a bigger house. It was about freedom. Freedom to choose how I spend my time, whom I spend it with, and how I shape my future. Money gives you options. That's its purpose.

The Cost of Misunderstanding Money

One of the clearest examples of misunderstanding money's purpose is what I call the **rat race**—that endless cycle of working harder and harder just to keep up with growing expenses. People get raises or bonuses, and what's the first thing they do? They upgrade their lifestyle. A better car, a bigger house, more expensive vacations. It's a trap that my dad warned me about time and time again. He used to say, *"It doesn't matter how much you make if you don't know how to keep it."*

I've watched so many people fall into this trap. It starts with a raise, a promotion, or even a lucky windfall. Instead of using that extra income to invest in their future, they spend it on more stuff. And that stuff comes with ongoing costs: higher insurance premiums, maintenance, property taxes. Soon, they find themselves working even harder just to maintain the lifestyle they've created. It's a cycle that's difficult to break once you're in it.

Dad's solution was simple: understand the real cost of every financial decision you make. He used to say, *"Before you buy something, ask yourself: Is this bringing you closer to the life you want, or is it just weighing you down?"* That question helped me avoid a lot of poor financial decisions, and it's one I still use today.

The Psychological Side of Money

One of the most important lessons I learned from Dad was that how we think about money can be just as important as how we earn or spend it. Money is deeply tied to our emotions. For some, it's a source of pride, for others, a source of anxiety. But Dad always approached money calmly, as if it were just a part of life—not something to fear or idolize.

He used to say, *"The moment you let money control how you feel, you've lost control over it."* And he was right. I've seen people stressed out because they don't have enough, and I've seen people just as stressed out because they're terrified of losing what they have. In both cases, money is in the driver's seat. They're not in control.

The key, Dad taught me, is to take the emotion out of money decisions. He didn't mean to stop caring about your financial future; rather, he meant that you need to approach money logically. If you get emotional about every decision—whether it's fear, greed, or envy—you'll end up making poor choices. But when you treat money like a tool, you can approach it calmly and make decisions that are aligned with your long-term goals.

Actionable Steps for Understanding Your Money Mindset

Assess Your Emotional Relationship with Money

The first step toward changing how you think about money is recognizing the emotional patterns you associate with it. Do you feel anxious when you think about your finances? Do you avoid checking your bank account because of fear or shame? Understanding these patterns will help you begin shifting your mindset.

Set Clear Financial Goals

What do you actually want from your money? This is a question Dad would ask me often. Not *"How much do you want?"* but rather, *"What kind of life do you want your money to help create?"* Is it more time with family? The ability to travel? Early retirement? When you understand what you're working toward, money becomes a means to an end, not the end itself.

Create a Spending Philosophy

This was something Dad was strict about. He had a clear spending philosophy that guided every financial decision. Before making a purchase, ask yourself, *"Does this bring me closer to my goals, or is it just satisfying a temporary desire?"* Developing your own philosophy about money can help prevent impulse spending and ensure that your financial decisions are always aligned with your long-term objectives.

Shifting the Mindset: From Consumer to Builder

Dad's biggest lesson on money was about shifting from a consumer mindset to a builder's mindset. Consumers use money to buy things. Builders use money to create opportunities. If you're always focused on what money can buy, you're missing out on what money can build. That was a critical shift for me, and it's one I hope you'll make as you go through this book.

When you start viewing money as a tool for creating opportunities—whether that's starting a business, investing in assets, or buying your time back—you'll find that your relationship with money starts to change. You stop chasing it. Instead, you start using it strategically, directing it toward things that will make your life better in the long run.

This shift doesn't happen overnight. It's a process of continually reminding yourself what money is for, and how it can serve your life, not dominate it. But once you make that shift, you'll find that you have more control over your financial future than you ever thought possible.

⌘⌘⌘

Understanding the true purpose of money is the foundation of everything else in this book. Until you get this right, no amount of saving, investing, or earning will bring you the freedom you're looking for. Money is a tool, not the destination. It's there to give you choices, to provide security, and to build a life that reflects your values—not the other way around.

Once you understand this, the rest of Dad's rules will fall into place. In the next chapter, we'll dive into the importance of saving, but with a twist:

It's not just about tucking money away. It's about building a financial foundation that allows you to start investing in your future—and in yourself.

Let's continue this journey together.

CHAPTER 2

RULE 2: SAVE, BUT DON'T JUST SAVE: BUILD YOUR FINANCIAL BASE

"If you only save money, you'll always be one step away from losing it. But if you build a financial base, you'll have a foundation that keeps growing, even when life throws you curveballs."

This is one of the first lessons Dad taught me about money. Saving was important, sure—but it wasn't enough. Dad would always say, *"Saving is step one, but don't stop there. What you do with that savings is what counts."* I didn't fully grasp this idea when I was younger. To me, saving was the ultimate sign of being responsible with money. If I had enough in my bank account, I'd be safe, right?

But Dad had a bigger vision. Saving, he explained, was just a starting point. The real goal was to build a financial base that could withstand the ups and downs of life, grow on its own, and serve as the springboard for future investments. This base, as Dad described it, wasn't just about stashing money away—it was about using that money to create stability, freedom, and eventually, wealth.

Why Saving Alone Isn't Enough

One of the biggest financial myths is that simply saving money will lead to financial security. It's a good start, but it's not the whole story. In fact, saving alone can leave you vulnerable. Why? Because money in a savings account doesn't grow. It sits there, losing value to inflation, while opportunities for building wealth pass by. That was a lesson I learned early on.

I remember when I got my first real job. I was so proud of the little savings I had managed to accumulate over the years. Every time I got paid, I would squirrel away a portion of my paycheck into a savings account. It felt like I was doing everything right. But Dad, as always, had a way of opening my eyes to the bigger picture.

He sat me down one day and asked, *"What's your plan for that money?"* I was confused—wasn't I already doing the responsible thing by saving it? He smiled and said, *"Saving is good, but it's just one part of the puzzle. If you only save, you're missing out on what that money could do for you."*

Dad explained that while saving helps you prepare for emergencies and gives you a sense of security, it doesn't grow your wealth. The real key was to use those savings as a base for something bigger—something that could grow on its own. That's when he introduced me to the idea of **building a financial foundation**.

Building Your Financial Base: The Four Pillars

A solid financial base isn't just about having money sitting in a bank. It's about structuring your finances in a way that provides security, opportunity, and growth. Dad broke it down into four key pillars, each one essential to creating a foundation that could support future wealth:

1. **Emergency Fund**
2. **Sinking Funds**
3. **Short-Term Savings for Goals**
4. **Investments That Grow**

These four elements combined create a financial base that can weather life's uncertainties, while still allowing room for growth and opportunity. Let's break them down.

Emergency Fund: Your Safety Net

Dad was a big believer in always being prepared for the unexpected. Life, as he liked to remind me, doesn't follow our plans. Jobs get lost, medical emergencies happen, cars break down. Having an emergency fund was non-negotiable for him. *"If you don't have a safety net,"* he said, *"you'll fall hard when life throws something unexpected at you."*

The emergency fund is the cornerstone of your financial base. It's not meant to grow wealth; it's meant to protect you from having to go into debt or liquidate investments when an unexpected expense pops up. This fund should be liquid—meaning easily accessible—and cover at least three to six months of living expenses.

But here's the key: once your emergency fund is set, you stop adding to it. This is where people sometimes get stuck. They focus on building a massive savings account without realizing that after a certain point, it's counterproductive. The emergency fund is there to protect, not to grow. Once it's in place, it's time to move on to other pillars.

Sinking Funds: Planning for Known Expenses

Sinking funds are another tool Dad taught me to use early on. These are savings accounts for known future expenses—things like car maintenance, home repairs, vacations, or holiday gifts. The idea is to break big expenses into smaller, manageable amounts that you can set aside over time, instead of being caught off guard when they come due.

For example, if you know you'll need $1,200 for car repairs in the next year, you'd divide that amount by 12 and save $100 a month. By the time the expense rolls around, you're ready for it. Dad called this *"predicting the future"* with money—it's about taking control of expenses before they control you.

Sinking funds take the stress out of big purchases and allow you to plan ahead without feeling like you're scrambling for cash when the time comes. And the best part? Since these funds are for specific purposes, you don't touch them until they're needed. That keeps your emergency fund intact for real emergencies.

Short-Term Savings: Working Toward Specific Goals

The third pillar of your financial base is short-term savings for specific goals. Unlike sinking funds, which are for predictable expenses, short-term savings are for discretionary goals—things like buying a new car, a down payment on a home, or even starting a business. These are larger, planned goals that don't necessarily fall under day-to-day living expenses.

Dad always said, *"If you don't have something you're working toward, you'll find yourself spending without purpose."* Short-term savings give your money a direction, a goal to work toward. Having these goals in place can motivate you to save and prevent you from making impulsive purchases that detract from your bigger financial picture.

The beauty of short-term savings is that it's flexible. You can prioritize different goals depending on your stage in life. The important thing is to be intentional with your savings and direct it toward things that bring you closer to financial independence.

Investments That Grow: Turning Savings into Wealth

This is where things start to get exciting. Once your emergency fund, sinking funds, and short-term savings are in place, it's time to put your money to work. Dad was clear about this: *"Your savings won't grow unless you invest them in something that does."*

Investing is the key to building long-term wealth. Whether it's through stocks, real estate, or your own business, investing allows your money to grow beyond what you could achieve through saving alone. Dad wasn't afraid of risk, but he always approached it carefully. *"The key is to invest in what you understand,"* he'd say. He wasn't about chasing the next big trend or trying to get rich quick. Instead, he focused on consistent, reliable growth.

The earlier you start investing, the more powerful the effects of compound interest will be. Even small amounts, when invested wisely, can grow significantly over time. Dad's approach was simple: save first, invest second. Once you've laid your financial foundation with the other pillars, you can start directing money into investments that will build wealth for the long term.

The Mindset Shift: Saving with Purpose

Saving for the sake of saving isn't the goal. Dad taught me that every dollar I saved should have a purpose. Whether it's for emergencies, planned expenses, or future investments, each pillar of your financial base is designed to support the bigger picture of financial independence.

This mindset shift—saving with purpose—was a game-changer for me. It took saving from something passive and turned it into an active, intentional process. Instead of just watching my savings account balance grow, I began to see those savings as the building blocks of a foundation that would give me freedom, stability, and opportunity.

And once that base was in place, I could start focusing on what came next: growing my wealth through investments, and eventually, using that wealth to buy my time back.

⌘⌘⌘

Building a financial base is about more than just saving money—it's about creating a foundation that supports your future. With the four pillars of an emergency fund, sinking funds, short-term savings, and investments, you're not just saving for a rainy day—you're saving with a strategy that sets you up for long-term success.

In the next chapter, we'll explore the most important investment you can ever make: the investment in yourself. As Dad always said, *"The best money you'll ever spend is on your own growth."* Let's dive into how personal development is the true key to unlocking your financial potential.

Chapter 3

Rule 3: Invest in Yourself Before Anything Else

"If you don't invest in yourself first, you'll never know how much you're truly capable of."

This was one of Dad's favorite sayings, and it's one that took me the longest to fully understand. When we think about investing, we often picture stocks, real estate, or businesses—anything that promises a financial return. But Dad's view was different. He believed that before you can invest in anything external, you need to first invest in your most important asset: yourself.

I didn't appreciate this at first. I was always focused on the numbers—how much I could save, how I could grow my money, and where I could invest to get the best returns. But over time, I realized that no investment, no matter how smart or lucrative, could outshine the benefits of investing in your own growth. Whether it's acquiring new skills, expanding your knowledge, or taking care of your health, every step you take to improve yourself has a ripple effect on your financial future.

The Power of Personal Development

Dad wasn't a wealthy man in the traditional sense. He didn't have a high-paying job, a fancy title, or a degree from a prestigious university. What he did have was an insatiable desire to learn and grow. He understood that in order to increase his value in the world, he needed to continually invest in his own knowledge and skills. This mindset shaped the way I approached my own personal and professional development.

Dad used to tell me, *"Your mind is the one thing no one can take away from you."* He believed that knowledge and skills were the greatest tools for building a better life—not just financially, but in every aspect of life. When you invest in yourself, you're not just increasing your earning potential; you're also creating opportunities that you wouldn't have had otherwise.

In a way, personal development is the ultimate form of compounding interest. The more you learn, the more opportunities you create for yourself, and the more those opportunities open up new paths for growth. Whether it's learning a new skill, starting a new project, or taking care of your mental and physical health, every step you take toward personal improvement multiplies your potential for success.

Building the Right Skills: Your Greatest Asset

When Dad talked about investing in yourself, he didn't mean only formal education, though he believed in its value. For him, it was about learning the skills that mattered most for your goals. Dad always had a book in his hands, and it wasn't always about business or finances—it was about anything that could make him better, more knowledgeable, or more capable of taking control of his future.

In my own journey, I realized that this advice was key to navigating the changing world around me. In today's fast-paced economy, the most successful people aren't just those with the best degrees or highest-paying jobs—they're the ones who are constantly learning, adapting, and evolving. The world changes fast, and if you're not learning, you're falling behind.

But here's where many people make a mistake: they focus too much on formal education and not enough on practical skills. It's not just about what you learn in school; it's about the real-world skills that make you more valuable in any setting. These might include:

- **Communication Skills**: Being able to express your ideas clearly and persuasively.

- **Problem-Solving Abilities**: Tackling challenges head-on and finding creative solutions.

- **Technical or Industry-Specific Knowledge**: Staying up-to-date on the latest tools, software, and developments in your field.

- **Financial Literacy**: Understanding how to manage your own money, as well as how to make smart investment decisions.

Dad believed that when you invest in developing these kinds of skills, you're not just making yourself more employable—you're making yourself indispensable. And that's where the real returns come in. Skills are the foundation of opportunity, and opportunity is the key to building wealth.

Investing in Your Health: The Hidden Wealth

One thing Dad stressed that isn't always mentioned in personal finance books was the importance of investing in your health. *"What's the point of building wealth,"* he would say, *"if you're too sick to enjoy it?"*

For Dad, physical and mental health were just as important as financial health. He believed that if you didn't take care of your body and mind, everything else would eventually fall apart. It's easy to get caught up in chasing wealth, working long hours, and sacrificing sleep or self-care in the name of progress. But without your health, all the money in the world is meaningless.

Dad lived by example. He wasn't a fitness fanatic, but he made sure to stay active, eat well, and maintain a balanced lifestyle. He believed that discipline in taking care of your health directly translated to discipline in your financial life. When you're healthy, you think clearer, make better decisions, and have the energy to pursue your goals. That's why investing in your health is, in many ways, an investment in your financial future.

Take Risks on Yourself: Entrepreneurship and Innovation

Another major area where Dad encouraged self-investment was in entrepreneurship. He wasn't a businessman in the traditional sense, but he understood the value of creating something of your own. He often said, *"The biggest risk you'll ever take is not on the stock market—it's on yourself."*

Dad believed in calculated risks, especially when it came to pursuing new ideas or business ventures. He'd ask, *"If you don't bet on yourself, why should anyone else?"* It took me a while to really understand that the biggest opportunities for growth come from taking control of your own destiny. Whether that means starting a business, launching a side project, or simply stepping outside of your comfort zone, investing in your own potential can lead to far greater rewards than playing it safe.

This idea is especially relevant today. The traditional model of working for someone else your whole life and retiring with a pension isn't as secure as it once was. Job security is no longer guaranteed, and the people who thrive are often those who create their own opportunities. Dad always encouraged me to think about ways I could turn my skills and passions into something that could generate income and independence. It wasn't about quitting my job and becoming an entrepreneur overnight—it was about constantly thinking about how I could add value and create opportunities for myself.

Actionable Steps for Investing in Yourself

Identify Your Skill Gaps

Take an honest look at where you are now and where you want to go. What skills do you need to get there? Whether it's improving your communication, learning how to manage your time better, or developing new technical expertise, knowing where you need to grow is the first step.

Commit to Lifelong Learning

Dad believed in learning something new every day. Whether it's through books, online courses, podcasts, or simply seeking out mentorship, you should always be feeding your mind. Make it a habit to dedicate time each week to personal growth.

Prioritize Your Health

Your health is your most important asset. Create habits that ensure you're taking care of both your physical and mental well-being. Exercise regularly, eat healthy, get enough sleep, and practice mindfulness or stress-relief techniques to keep your mind sharp.

Take Small Risks on Yourself

Invest in side projects or explore areas of interest that can eventually turn into income streams or new opportunities. It doesn't have to be a grand leap into entrepreneurship—small risks can lead to big rewards over time.

The Compounding Effect of Self-Investment

The beauty of investing in yourself is that it pays dividends in every area of your life. The skills you develop, the knowledge you acquire, and the health you maintain all contribute to your ability to earn more, work smarter, and live better. Over time, this self-investment compounds, much like financial investments do. The more you grow, the more opportunities you create for yourself—and the more prepared you are to seize those opportunities when they come your way.

Dad was right: the greatest investment you'll ever make is in yourself. And it's one that never stops paying off.

⌘⌘⌘

Investing in yourself is the foundation of everything else. Without it, all the money you save or invest won't reach its full potential. Your knowledge, skills, and health are your greatest assets—and they're the key to unlocking financial independence.

In the next chapter, we'll explore how to take the next step toward financial freedom:

understanding the power of assets vs. liabilities, and how to build a life where your money works for you, not the other way around.

CHAPTER 4

RULE 4: UNDERSTAND THE POWER OF ASSETS VS. LIABILITIES

Dad used to say, *"If you want to be financially free, you need to know the difference between an asset and a liability. Otherwise, you'll always feel like you're running in place."* He wasn't just talking about money—he was talking about how we choose to use our resources, time, and energy.

The concept of assets vs. liabilities is a simple one, but it's incredibly powerful. Once you understand the difference and start applying it to your life, you begin to see your financial situation in a whole new light. For Dad, this was one of the most important lessons he ever taught me about money: **assets put money in your pocket, liabilities take money out**.

It sounds obvious, right? But most people get this wrong. They think they're building wealth by acquiring things that actually drain their resources. The house you live in, the car you drive, the gadgets and clothes you buy—these might feel like symbols of success, but if they're not putting money back into your pocket, they're not assets.

The Misconception of Wealth

When I was younger, I thought wealth was about having more stuff. The bigger house, the fancier car, the newest technology—these were all signs that someone was financially successful. But Dad opened my eyes to a different way of thinking. He told me, *"Wealth isn't about how much you own, it's about how much your money is working for you."*

This was a hard pill to swallow at first. After all, society teaches us to equate success with possessions. But Dad's approach was different. He saw wealth not in the things people owned, but in the freedom their money gave them. And that freedom only came from owning things that generated more money—**assets**—instead of things that drained it—**liabilities**.

I remember the day he sat me down and walked me through his own financial journey. He didn't have a flashy lifestyle, but he had financial security. He didn't drive the newest car or live in a mansion, but he never worried about money. Why? Because he had built a life based on acquiring assets that worked for him. His focus wasn't on spending—it was on building.

What Is an Asset?

So what exactly is an asset? In the simplest terms, an asset is something that puts money into your pocket, either directly or indirectly. It can take many forms, but the key is that it generates income or increases in value over time. The more assets you own, the more financial freedom you have.

Here are some common examples of assets:

- **Real Estate**: Rental properties that generate income, or properties that appreciate in value over time.

- **Stocks and Bonds**: Investments that provide dividends or interest payments, and increase in value over the long term.

- **Businesses**: Either a business you own outright or a share of a business that generates profit.

- **Intellectual Property**: Books, patents, or other intellectual property that generates royalties or licensing fees.

- **Cash-Flow Investments**: These could include anything from peer-to-peer lending to owning a vending machine business— investments that provide regular, passive income.

It's important to note that not all of these assets are right for everyone. What's crucial is finding the assets that align with your skills, interests, and goals. Dad always said, *"Invest in what you understand."* If you don't understand an investment, you're taking a risk you're not prepared for.

What Is a Liability?

A liability, on the other hand, is something that takes money out of your pocket. These are the things that drain your resources, either by requiring constant payments or by losing value over time. The tricky part is that many liabilities **feel** like assets at first glance, because they give us a sense of achievement or success.

Here are some common examples of liabilities:

- **Your Home (if it doesn't generate income)**: A home you live in may seem like an asset, but unless it generates rental income or appreciates significantly in value, it's a liability due to mortgage payments, maintenance, and taxes.

- **Cars**: Even if you own your car outright, it still requires insurance, fuel, and maintenance. And cars depreciate quickly, meaning they lose value over time.

- **Consumer Debt**: Credit cards, personal loans, or any other kind of debt that you're paying interest on are major liabilities. They eat away at your financial stability.

- **Luxury Goods**: Expensive clothing, gadgets, or anything else that doesn't increase in value. These items may give you temporary satisfaction but contribute nothing to your long-term wealth.

The biggest mistake people make is assuming that just because they own something, it's an asset. But if it's costing you money every month without giving anything back, it's a liability. And if your life is full of liabilities, you'll find it very difficult to achieve financial independence.

Shifting Your Focus: Acquiring More Assets

One of the most transformative pieces of advice Dad gave me was to **stop focusing on acquiring stuff** and start focusing on acquiring assets. This shift in thinking completely changed how I viewed my financial future. It wasn't about how much I could earn or save anymore—it was about how much I could invest in things that would grow.

Dad had a very straightforward approach to this. He believed that once you understood the power of assets, every financial decision you made should be measured by this question: **Is this putting money into my pocket or taking it out?**

For example:

- Instead of buying a second car, he might look at buying a rental property.

- Instead of splurging on a luxury vacation, he'd invest that money in stocks that paid dividends.

- Instead of upgrading to a bigger house, he might invest in a business that would generate passive income.

This wasn't about deprivation—it was about building. He wasn't denying himself the good things in life, but he always made sure his financial decisions were aligned with his long-term goals of wealth creation and financial freedom.

Turning Your Liabilities Into Assets

The good news is that you don't have to live without nice things. The key is learning how to turn liabilities into assets, or at the very least, make sure your liabilities don't drain your wealth over the long term.

Here are a few ways Dad taught me to think about this:

1. **House Hacking**: If you own a home, can you rent out a portion of it (a room, basement, or

separate unit) to generate income? This turns your home from a liability into an asset.

2. **Car Sharing**: If you own a car, can you rent it out when you're not using it? There are services that allow you to earn money by renting your car to others, reducing its liability.

3. **Monetizing Hobbies**: If you spend money on a hobby, can you find a way to turn that hobby into an income stream? For example, if you love photography, can you sell your photos or offer services for hire?

4. **Business Use of Property**: Can you use part of your home for a business? Whether it's starting a small online business or consulting, using your property to generate income turns it into more of an asset.

Dad was always thinking creatively about how to make the most out of what he already had. His approach wasn't about cutting costs to the bone—it was about maximizing the potential of everything he owned.

The Snowball Effect of Assets

The beauty of acquiring assets is that the more you accumulate, the more they begin to work together, creating what Dad called a *"snowball effect."* Once you have a base of income-generating assets, you can reinvest the money they produce into acquiring more assets. This creates a cycle where your wealth builds on itself, growing faster and faster over time.

For example:

- You might start with a small rental property. Over time, the rental income you earn allows you to buy more properties.

- Your stock portfolio may start small, but as you reinvest dividends and buy more shares, it grows exponentially.

- A small side business can eventually grow into a full-time income stream, giving you the freedom to invest more in other areas.

The key is patience and consistency. Wealth doesn't happen overnight, but if you focus on acquiring and growing assets, the snowball effect will eventually lead to financial freedom.

⌘⌘⌘

Understanding the difference between assets and liabilities is one of the most important lessons you can learn about money. Once you start thinking of your financial decisions in these terms, you'll see the world differently. Your focus will shift from acquiring things that drain your resources to building a portfolio of assets that create opportunities and freedom.

In the next chapter, we'll dive deeper into another critical aspect of financial independence: creating multiple income streams. As Dad often said, *"Don't put all your eggs in one basket—find more baskets."* Let's explore how to diversify your income and build security in the face of an unpredictable world.

CHAPTER 5

RULE 5: THE IMPORTANCE OF CREATING MULTIPLE INCOME STREAMS

"If all your eggs are in one basket, it only takes one stumble to lose everything."

This was one of Dad's most crucial rules. Growing up, I remember him always having multiple projects going on—whether it was a side gig, a small investment, or a new idea he was exploring. He didn't rely on a single source of income, and that strategy became his secret to financial security. It's a lesson that has only become more relevant in today's world.

The job market is unpredictable, the economy can shift without warning, and relying solely on a paycheck from one employer can leave you vulnerable. That's why Dad always preached the importance of diversifying income streams. *"If one dries up, the others will keep you afloat,"* he used to say.

But creating multiple income streams isn't just about protecting yourself from risk—it's also one of the fastest ways to build wealth and achieve financial independence. Each income stream can contribute to your financial foundation, helping you grow your assets, pay off liabilities, and move closer to the freedom you're working toward.

Why Relying on One Income Is Risky

For many years, the traditional model of earning a living was simple: Get a job, work hard, save for retirement, and you'll be fine. But things have changed. Job security isn't what it used to be, and depending on a single paycheck can be dangerous. If that income disappears—whether because of layoffs, health issues, or a company shutting down—you're left scrambling.

Dad experienced this firsthand when the company he worked for downsized during an economic recession. He had worked there for years, climbing the ladder and relying on his steady paycheck to support our family. But when the layoffs came, it was a shock. Suddenly, the security of his job was gone. What saved us was the fact that Dad had been building multiple streams of income on the side for years.

He had small investments in stocks, a rental property generating income, and a side business that allowed him to make ends meet while he searched for another job. While many of his colleagues were struggling to pay their bills, Dad's diversified income streams gave our family a safety net. It was a lesson I never forgot.

The Types of Income Streams

There are many ways to create multiple income streams, and you don't need to be wealthy or have a lot of capital to start. In fact, most people can begin with what they already have or know. Dad broke down income streams into two categories: **active income** and **passive income**.

- **Active Income**: This is money you earn by trading your time and effort. Your primary job, freelance work, consulting, or side hustles all fall into this category. The key with active income is that it typically requires ongoing involvement to generate money.

- **Passive Income**: This is income that continues to flow after the initial work has been done. While passive income streams often require an upfront investment of time, money, or effort, they eventually generate income with little day-to-day involvement.

Examples include rental properties, dividends from stocks, royalties from books or intellectual property, and automated online businesses.

The magic of multiple income streams comes when you begin to mix active and passive sources, allowing you to grow your income even while you sleep.

Building Your First Income Stream

For most people, their primary source of income is their job or career. This is usually the biggest, most reliable stream of income, and it forms the foundation of your financial life. But if you want to build financial independence, it can't be the only one.

So how do you get started with creating additional income streams? The first step is to look at your current situation and identify where you have untapped potential. Dad always encouraged me to think creatively about how I could use my existing skills, resources, and interests to create new income opportunities.

Here are some common ways to begin diversifying your income:

1. **Start a Side Hustle**

   A side hustle is one of the easiest ways to generate active income outside of your primary job. It can be something you're passionate about or a skill you already have. For example, freelance writing, graphic design, tutoring, or even selling products online. The internet has made it easier than ever to turn hobbies or talents into additional income streams.

2. **Freelance or Consult**

   If you have specialized knowledge in your field, consider freelancing or offering consulting services. Many companies are willing to pay for expertise on a short-term basis without committing to a full-time employee. Consulting can be a great way to generate income while maintaining your regular job.

3. **Invest in Dividend Stocks**

Stocks that pay dividends provide regular passive income while also allowing your investment to grow over time. Dividends are a share of the company's profits paid out to investors, and if you reinvest them, you can increase your ownership in the company, leading to even more passive income.

4. **Real Estate Investment**

Owning rental properties can be one of the most lucrative ways to generate passive income. While real estate requires upfront investment and some ongoing management, it can provide a steady stream of cash flow through rental payments. As property values increase, your investment grows in value as well.

5. **Create Digital Products**

Digital products like eBooks, online courses, or apps can generate passive income once they're created. The beauty of digital products is that they can be sold over and over again with very little additional effort. If you have expertise in a certain area, consider creating a product that others can benefit from.

Diversifying Into Passive Income

While side hustles and freelance work are great ways to boost your income, the real key to financial independence is generating passive income. Passive income streams allow you to build wealth without having to constantly trade your time for money. Dad always said, *"If you can find a way to earn money while you sleep, you're on the right track."*

Here are a few ways to create passive income:

1. Rental Properties

One of Dad's favorite passive income strategies was real estate. If you buy a rental property and manage it well, you can earn steady income from rent while your property appreciates in value. The trick is to buy properties that generate more in rent than they cost in mortgage payments, taxes, and maintenance. Over time, the rental income can grow, and the property itself becomes an asset that increases your net worth.

2. **Peer-to-Peer Lending**

Peer-to-peer lending platforms allow you to lend money to individuals or small businesses in exchange for interest payments. While this carries some risk, it can also provide higher returns than traditional savings accounts or bonds. The key is to diversify your lending across many borrowers to spread the risk.

3. **Royalties from Creative Work**

If you've created something of value, such as a book, song, or patent, you can earn royalties each time it's sold or used. This is the ultimate form of passive income because you do the work once and continue earning for years. Dad always encouraged me to think about how I could create something that would continue generating income long after the work was done.

4. Automated Online Business

Many online businesses can be set up to generate passive income. For example, if you create an online store that sells digital products, once it's up and running, the sales process can be automated. You earn money from sales without needing to be actively involved in day-to-day operations. Dad was always fascinated by the power of automation, and today's technology makes it easier than ever to build an online business that runs itself.

Combining Income Streams for Financial Independence

The goal isn't just to have one or two extra income streams—it's to build enough streams that together, they give you financial security and freedom. Dad liked to think of it as *"financial insulation."* When you have multiple income streams, you insulate yourself from risk. If one stream dries up or decreases, you have others to fall back on.

Imagine this: You have a full-time job that covers your living expenses. On top of that, you have a rental property that generates monthly cash flow, stocks that pay quarterly dividends, and a side hustle that brings in additional active income. Each of these streams may not be enough to support you on its own, but combined, they create a powerful financial engine.

This is the path to financial independence. It's not about getting rich quick or relying on a single source of income to carry you through life. It's about creating a diversified financial foundation that can weather the ups and downs of the economy, job market, and your personal circumstances.

Actionable Steps for Building Multiple Income Streams

Start Small

You don't need to build five income streams overnight. Start with one—whether it's a side hustle, a small investment, or a digital product.

Once that income stream is up and running, move on to the next one.

Diversify Wisely

Don't put all your energy into one type of income stream. If your job is your primary active income, consider adding a passive income stream like investments or rental properties. Diversification is key to long-term stability.

Reinvest Your Profits

As you start generating additional income, reinvest it into growing your assets. Use your side hustle income to buy dividend-paying stocks, or invest the profits from a rental property into another property. This accelerates the growth of your income streams.

Automate Where Possible

Look for ways to automate parts of your income streams. Whether it's setting up an automated investment plan, creating a passive online business, or outsourcing tasks in your side hustle Automation is a powerful tool for creating sustainable income streams without requiring constant time and attention. For example, you can set up automatic investments into index funds, use online platforms to manage rental properties, or use software to automate an online business. The less time you need to spend managing your income streams, the more freedom you gain to focus on other opportunities or simply enjoy life.

Track Your Progress

One of the keys to building multiple income streams is tracking how each one performs. Set up a system to monitor how much each stream is bringing in, how much time and effort it requires, and what you can do to optimize or grow it. Dad used to say, "If you're not measuring it, you're not managing it." Keep an eye on your progress and adjust your strategy as needed to ensure your income streams are working together to build your financial independence.

The Power of Multiple Streams: Security and Freedom

Dad's philosophy on creating multiple income streams wasn't just about protecting yourself from risk—it was about creating the freedom to live life on your own terms. When you have diversified sources of income, you're no longer dependent on any one job or business to sustain you. This provides both security and flexibility, two of the most valuable things you can have in life.

I remember when I reached a point in my own financial journey where my income streams allowed me to make choices based on what I wanted, rather than what I needed to do to pay the bills. That's the kind of freedom Dad always talked about. It wasn't just about having more money—it was about having control over your time, your decisions, and your life.

One of the most liberating moments for me was realizing that I didn't need to stress about my job the way I used to. If something happened and I lost my main source of income, I had backup streams that would keep me afloat. That peace of mind was worth more than any paycheck.

The other great advantage of multiple income streams is that they create more opportunities for growth. Once you're generating income from different sources, you can reinvest those profits into new ventures, building wealth at a faster rate than relying on a single income. This is how the wealthy build their fortunes—not through one paycheck, but through many different channels working together.

Balancing Time and Effort Across Income Streams

Of course, creating multiple income streams doesn't mean burning yourself out. Dad was always careful to balance his time between his main job, his side projects, and his personal life. He understood that while building wealth was important, it shouldn't come at the cost of his health or relationships.

The key is to find a balance that works for you. You don't need to spend all your free time hustling, but you should make a habit of investing time and energy into your income streams consistently. Start small, focus on what you can manage, and grow from there. As your income streams mature, you'll find that some require less effort than others, allowing you to focus more on growth and reinvestment.

Automation and delegation can also help here. If a side hustle or passive income stream is taking up too much of your time, look for ways to streamline it. Can you hire someone to help manage certain aspects of it? Can you use technology to automate some of the processes? The goal is to create a system where your income streams are working for you, not the other way around.

Action Plan: Get Started on Your First Additional Income Stream

Let's break down the steps to help you start building your first additional income stream today:

1. **Evaluate Your Current Skills and Interests**

   Think about what you're good at and what you enjoy doing. Your first additional income stream could be something that leverages your current expertise or hobbies. This will make it easier to get started and maintain momentum.

2. **Decide Between Active or Passive Income**

Consider whether you want to focus on active income (which requires ongoing work, like freelancing or side hustles) or passive income (which requires upfront effort but minimal ongoing management, like investments or digital products). Both have their benefits, and the best approach is often to combine the two.

3. **Research Opportunities**

Once you've identified what type of income stream you want to create, do your research. Look into different side hustles, investment opportunities, or digital products. There's a wealth of information available online, and the more you understand your options, the better decisions you'll make.

4. **Start Small and Scale**

You don't need to hit a home run right away. Start with a small side project, a small investment, or a digital product that doesn't require a large upfront commitment. Once you have your first income stream up and running, you can scale it over time and look for ways to grow or add more streams.

5. **Set a Timeline and Goals**

Set realistic goals for how much additional income you want to generate and a timeline for when you want to achieve it. Having clear goals will keep you focused and motivated as you build your new income streams.

⌘⌘⌘

Creating multiple income streams is one of the most powerful strategies for building financial independence. It provides security, protects you from life's uncertainties, and gives you the freedom to make decisions based on what you want, not what you need to survive. As you diversify your income and invest in growing your wealth, you'll begin to experience the financial freedom Dad always talked about.

In the next chapter, we'll explore the importance of patience and the long game. As Dad used to say, *"Building wealth isn't a sprint, it's a marathon."* We'll dive into the power of time and compound interest, and how a patient, steady approach to investing can yield incredible results.

CHAPTER 6

RULE 6: ALWAYS PLAY THE LONG GAME: PATIENCE, TIME, AND COMPOUND INTEREST

Dad was a big believer in patience. *"The long game always wins,"* he would say. For him, financial independence wasn't about quick wins or chasing short-term gains—it was about building wealth steadily, over time. This mindset shaped how he approached everything: investing, saving, and even spending. He understood that the key to true financial freedom wasn't trying to outsmart the market or get rich overnight—it was time.

I used to think Dad was being overly cautious. I wanted to see fast results, and I was constantly tempted by the idea of quick returns. But Dad had seen what happened when people got greedy or impatient. He knew that true wealth wasn't built in a year or even five years—it was built over decades. The secret? Letting your money work for you, slowly but surely, through the power of compound interest.

The Power of Patience

Patience is one of the most undervalued traits in personal finance. In a world where we're conditioned to expect instant gratification—whether it's through the latest technology, the fastest internet, or same-day delivery—it's easy to forget that some of the best things in life take time. Building wealth is one of them.

Dad's approach to money was always steady and measured. He didn't jump on the latest trends or gamble on risky investments. Instead, he focused on consistency. *"It's not about how much you make in the short term,"* he would say. *"It's about how much you keep, and how you let that grow over time."*

This mentality is especially important when it comes to investing. The stock market, real estate, and other investment vehicles can be unpredictable in the short term. There will be ups and downs, and it's easy to get emotional when you see your investments dip. But Dad always reminded me that the market rewards patience. Those who panic and pull out during a downturn often miss out on the long-term gains that come with staying the course.

Compound Interest: The Eighth Wonder of the World

One of the first things Dad taught me about money was the power of compound interest. He called it the *"eighth wonder of the world,"* echoing the famous quote attributed to Albert Einstein. The idea behind compound interest is simple but profound: it's the process of earning interest not just on your initial investment, but also on the interest that investment has already earned. In other words, your money starts making money, and that money makes more money, and so on. Over time, the growth becomes exponential.

I remember when Dad sat me down to show me how it worked. He pulled out a calculator and showed me two scenarios: one where I saved $100 a month and left it sitting in a regular savings account, and one where I invested $100 a month with a modest interest rate. The difference over 30 years was staggering. In the first case, I would have saved $36,000. In the second, I would have over $120,000, thanks to the magic of compound interest.

The beauty of compound interest is that it doesn't require you to have a lot of money to start. What it does require, however, is time and patience. The earlier you start, the more time your money has to grow. Dad used to say, *"Every year you wait to invest is a year you're missing out on free money."* He taught me that the most valuable thing you can give your investments is time.

Time in the Market Beats Timing the Market

One of the biggest mistakes people make when it comes to investing is trying to time the market—buying and selling based on short-term fluctuations, hoping to buy low and sell high. But even the most experienced investors will tell you that predicting the market is next to impossible. You might get lucky once or twice, but in the long run, trying to time the market is more likely to hurt than help.

Dad wasn't interested in chasing the next big stock or getting in on the latest trend. He believed in what's called **"time in the market."** The idea is simple: the longer your money is invested, the more opportunity it has to grow, regardless of the day-to-day or even year-to-year volatility of the market. The stock market, for example, has historically returned an average of 7-10% annually over long periods, despite short-term dips and crashes.

By staying invested and reinvesting dividends or earnings, you allow compound interest to work its magic. Even during market downturns, Dad would hold firm. *"The market always bounces back,"* he would say, and he was right. Over time, the market trends upward, and those who stay invested reap the rewards.

The Snowball Effect: Starting Small, Growing Big

One of the most important lessons Dad imparted to me was that it doesn't matter how small you start—what matters is that you start. I used to think I needed to have a lot of money to begin investing, but Dad showed me that even small amounts, invested consistently over time, can turn into something significant.

He often used the analogy of a snowball rolling down a hill. In the beginning, it starts small, but as it rolls, it picks up more snow, growing larger and larger. The same goes for your investments. In the early years, the growth may seem slow. But as your returns compound, the momentum builds. Before you know it, your snowball of wealth is rolling faster and faster, growing exponentially.

This is why starting early is so critical. The earlier you start investing, the more time you give your money to grow, and the bigger your snowball becomes. If you wait until later in life, you may have to invest significantly more to catch up. As Dad would say, *"Time is your greatest ally in building wealth."*

Consistency Over Perfection

One of the reasons people struggle with building wealth is because they're waiting for the "perfect" time to invest. They worry about market conditions, interest rates, or finding the "perfect" investment. But Dad had a different perspective: *"There's no perfect time. There's only today. If you keep waiting, you'll never start."*

He wasn't saying to be reckless or invest without understanding what you're doing. Rather, he believed that the most important thing was to start consistently investing, even if it was just a small amount. In his view, consistency beats perfection every time. By consistently investing over the years, you smooth out the ups and downs of the market and put yourself on the path to steady growth.

It's easy to get caught up in analysis paralysis, trying to find the ideal moment to invest or worrying that you'll make a mistake. But Dad's approach was simple: start with what you can, when you can, and stick with it. Over time, those small, consistent efforts will compound into something much larger.

Harnessing the Power of Time in Different Investments

Dad wasn't just talking about the stock market when he talked about playing the long game. His philosophy applied to all kinds of investments, including real estate, business ventures, and even personal development.

- **In Real Estate**: One of Dad's favorite sayings was, *"The best time to buy real estate was 10 years ago. The second best time is today."* He believed in holding onto properties for the long term, allowing their value to appreciate over time. Rental properties, in particular, provided steady cash flow, while the properties themselves increased in value.

- **In Business**: Dad also believed in taking a long-term view when it came to business. He wasn't interested in quick profits—he was interested in building something sustainable. He would invest time, money, and energy into ventures that had the potential to grow steadily over the years, knowing that slow and steady often wins the race.

- **In Personal Growth**: Playing the long game wasn't just about financial investments. Dad also applied this principle to self-development. He believed that personal growth—whether through education, skill-building, or health—required time and patience. The more you invest in yourself over the years, the more you'll be able to achieve later in life.

The Risks of Impatience and Short-Term Thinking

While patience can help you build wealth, impatience is one of the fastest ways to lose it. I saw this firsthand with friends who would jump on every new investment trend, hoping to make a quick profit. Sometimes they'd get lucky, but more often than not, they'd end up losing money, frustrated and disillusioned.

Dad always warned me about the dangers of short-term thinking. *"If you're chasing fast money, you'll never catch it,"* he'd say. In his view, financial independence was a long journey, not a sprint. The people who rush into investments looking for immediate returns often find themselves taking on too much risk or making poor decisions based on emotion rather than logic.

I've seen people panic and sell their investments during a market downturn, only to watch the market recover shortly after. I've seen others pile money into get-rich-quick schemes, only to lose everything when the scheme collapses. Patience, as Dad always reminded me, is a form of discipline. It requires you to keep your emotions in check, stay focused on your long-term goals, and trust that time will do its work.

Actionable Steps for Playing the Long Game

Start Now

No matter where you are financially, the best time to start investing is today. Don't wait for the "perfect" moment or for a large sum of money. Even small amounts, invested consistently over time, can grow significantly through the power of compound interest.

Invest for the Long Term

Choose investments with a long-term perspective. Focus on assets like stocks, real estate, or bonds that have a track record of growth over time. Avoid trying to time the market or jumping on speculative trends that promise quick gains.

Reinvest Your Earnings

One of the best ways to harness the power of compound interest is to reinvest any earnings, whether they come from dividends, interest, or rental income. Reinvesting allows your money to grow faster and accelerates the snowball effect.

Stay the Course

Resist the temptation to sell or change course based on short-term market fluctuations. As long as your investments are sound and aligned with your long-term goals, staying the course will allow you to benefit from market recoveries and long-term growth.

Patience and Discipline

Develop the mindset of patience and discipline. Trust in the long game, and remember that building wealth takes time. Focus on consistency and steady growth, rather than instant gratification.

⌘⌘⌘

Playing the long game is the key to financial independence. It's not about quick wins or trying to beat the market—it's about letting time and compound interest work in your favor. As Dad always said, *"Time is your best friend in building wealth. Don't waste it by being impatient."*

In the next chapter, we'll tackle another crucial element of financial independence: debt. We'll explore how to use debt wisely, when it can help you, and when it can hold you back. As Dad liked to say, *"Debt can be a tool or a trap—it's all in how you use it."*

Chapter 7

Rule 7: Smart Debt: When and How to Use Leverage

"If you don't control debt, it will control you."

This was one of Dad's firmest beliefs. To him, debt was a tool—one that could either build your financial future or destroy it, depending on how it was used. He never saw debt as something inherently bad, but he also didn't believe in using it recklessly. Instead, he had a clear philosophy: **there's good debt and bad debt**—and knowing the difference between the two is crucial for building wealth.

While some people treat debt like a burden to avoid at all costs, others take on too much and quickly find themselves in over their heads. Dad's approach was all about balance. He understood that debt, when used wisely, could be a powerful way to build assets, grow wealth, and achieve financial independence. But he also knew that when misused, it could trap people in a cycle of financial stress and dependency.

Understanding Good Debt vs. Bad Debt

The first lesson Dad taught me about debt was that not all debt is created equal. Some debt can be productive and help you build wealth, while other debt can drag you down and prevent you from moving forward. He broke it down into two categories:

- **Good Debt**: This is debt that helps you acquire assets or increase your income. It's debt that works for you rather than against you. Examples of good debt include mortgages on rental properties, business loans that allow you to expand a profitable venture, or student loans (if they result in a higher earning potential).

- **Bad Debt**: This is debt that drains your resources without adding value. It's usually tied to liabilities rather than assets—things like credit card debt, personal loans for consumer goods, or auto loans for cars that quickly depreciate in value. Bad debt takes money out of your pocket and makes it harder to build wealth.

For Dad, the difference between good and bad debt came down to one simple question: **Is this debt helping you make more money, or is it costing you more than it's worth?**

How Good Debt Can Build Wealth

When used strategically, debt can be a powerful tool for wealth-building. The key is to use it in a way that generates income or increases the value of your assets. Dad was a master of leveraging good debt to build financial security. He understood that borrowing money wasn't inherently risky—it was what you did with that money that mattered.

Here are a few ways Dad taught me to use good debt wisely:

1. **Real Estate**

   One of the most common ways to use good debt is through real estate investing. A mortgage on a rental property, for example, can be a form of good debt because the property generates rental income that covers the mortgage and other expenses. Over time, the property appreciates in value, and the rental income continues to flow, creating passive income and building wealth. In this case, the debt is working for you.

2. Business Loans

If you own a business, taking out a loan to expand your operations can be a smart use of debt—**if** that loan helps you increase profits. For example, borrowing money to open a second location or invest in new equipment might allow you to serve more customers and generate higher revenue. In this case, the debt is used to grow an asset that increases your overall income.

3. Education Loans

While student loans often get a bad reputation, they can be a form of good debt—**if** they lead to higher earning potential. Dad's rule was simple: only take on education debt if the degree or training you're pursuing will significantly increase your ability to earn. Borrowing money to pursue a degree in a high-demand field with strong job prospects can be a good investment in your future. However, taking on large loans for a degree that doesn't improve your earning potential falls into the bad debt category.

4. Investment in Yourself

Sometimes, good debt is about taking a calculated risk to invest in your own skills, knowledge, or abilities. For example, if you need to borrow money to start a side hustle or build an online course that generates passive income, that debt could pay off in the long run. The key is to ensure that the investment has a clear path to increasing your income or building an asset.

The Trap of Bad Debt

On the flip side, bad debt can be a major obstacle to financial independence. While it's often tempting to finance things that bring immediate satisfaction—like a new car, the latest gadgets, or even vacations—this type of debt rarely adds long-term value. Instead, it creates a burden that can take years to pay off, all while costing you in interest payments and limiting your ability to invest in things that actually build wealth.

Dad always had a rule: **if it's not going to increase in value or generate income, don't go into debt for it.**

Here are some of the most common forms of bad debt:

1. **Credit Card Debt**

   Credit cards are one of the easiest ways to accumulate bad debt. With high interest rates and minimum payments that barely make a dent in the balance, it's easy for credit card debt to spiral out of control. If you're using credit cards to buy things you can't afford to pay off right away—like clothes, electronics, or meals out—you're setting yourself up for financial stress down the line.

2. **Car Loans**

   While it's true that cars are a necessity for many people, financing a car with a large loan is often a form of bad debt. Cars depreciate in value the moment you drive them off the lot, and the monthly payments can take a big chunk out of your budget. Dad always believed in buying used cars with cash, if possible, or taking out the smallest loan possible and paying it off quickly.

3. **Personal Loans for Consumer Goods**

Whether it's a loan for a new home entertainment system, a vacation, or expensive furniture, personal loans for consumer goods fall firmly into the bad debt category. These items lose value quickly, and the interest you pay on the loan will end up costing you much more than the item is worth.

4. **Payday Loans**

Payday loans are one of the worst forms of bad debt. With sky-high interest rates and short repayment terms, they trap borrowers in a cycle of debt that's difficult to escape. Dad always said, "If you need a payday loan, something's gone wrong with your financial planning." The best way to avoid payday loans is to build an emergency fund and budget carefully so you're not caught off guard by unexpected expenses.

Using Debt Wisely: Dad's Rules for Leverage

Dad had a few key rules when it came to using debt as a tool for building wealth. These rules helped him avoid the pitfalls of bad debt while taking advantage of the opportunities that good debt could provide.

1. **Only Borrow What You Can Repay**

   One of the biggest mistakes people make is borrowing more than they can realistically afford to repay. This often leads to missed payments, accumulating interest, and mounting debt. Dad always believed in borrowing conservatively—whether it was a mortgage, business loan, or education loan. He would run the numbers, make sure the payments fit comfortably within his budget, and never stretch himself too thin.

2. **Have a Clear Plan for Repayment**

   Before taking on any debt, Dad always made sure he had a solid repayment plan in place. Whether it was a mortgage, a business loan, or an investment in a rental property, he would calculate how long it would take to pay off the debt, how much interest he'd be paying, and whether the investment was worth the cost. Having a clear plan for how you'll repay the debt is crucial for using it wisely.

3. **Make Debt Work for You**

If Dad was going to take on debt, it was always with the goal of making that debt work for him. He would ask, "How is this debt going to help me make more money?" If the debt wasn't directly contributing to building an asset or increasing his income, he wouldn't take it on. For example, a mortgage on a rental property or a business loan that allowed him to expand his operations made sense because they would pay off in the long run.

4. **Pay Down High-Interest Debt First**

If you find yourself with both good and bad debt, Dad's advice was always to focus on paying down high-interest debt first—especially credit card debt or payday loans. The longer you carry high-interest debt, the more it costs you. By aggressively paying off these debts, you free up more money to invest in things that will actually build wealth.

5. Avoid Debt for Depreciating Assets

One of Dad's biggest rules was to never go into debt for something that would lose value over time. Whether it was a car, furniture, or expensive electronics, Dad believed that if you couldn't pay for it in cash, you shouldn't buy it. Taking out a loan for something that depreciates in value means you're paying more for an item that's worth less and less as time goes on.

Actionable Steps for Using Debt Wisely

Audit Your Current Debts

Take a close look at the debt you currently have. Which debts are helping you build assets or increase your income? Which debts are draining your resources without adding value? Make a plan to pay off any bad debt as quickly as possible, starting with the highest-interest loans.

Develop a Debt Repayment Strategy

If you have multiple debts, develop a strategy for paying them down. The **debt snowball** method (paying off the smallest balances first) can provide quick wins and motivation, while the **debt avalanche** method (paying off the highest-interest debt first) can save you more money in the long run. Whichever method you choose, stay consistent and focused on eliminating bad debt.

Use Debt for Income-Generating Assets Only

Before taking on new debt, ask yourself whether this debt will help you acquire an asset that generates income or appreciates in value. If it doesn't, reconsider whether you really need it. Avoid debt for liabilities or depreciating assets like cars, consumer goods, or non-essential purchases.

Establish an Emergency Fund to Avoid Future Debt

One of the best ways to avoid falling into bad debt is to have an emergency fund in place. By saving three to six months' worth of living expenses, you'll have a safety net in case of unexpected financial emergencies, reducing the need to rely on high-interest credit cards or loans.

Learn to Live Below Your Means

The simplest way to stay out of bad debt is to live within your means. This doesn't mean living a life of deprivation, but rather making intentional financial choices that prioritize saving and investing over unnecessary spending. As Dad used to say, *"You can't build wealth if you're spending it faster than you're earning it."*

The Role of Debt in Financial Independence

When used correctly, debt can be a stepping stone to financial independence. Dad's approach to debt wasn't about avoiding it entirely—it was about using it as a strategic tool. Good debt can help you acquire assets, start businesses, and build a foundation for long-term wealth. But bad debt can quickly undermine those efforts and trap you in a cycle of financial stress.

The key is understanding when and how to use debt to your advantage. By leveraging good debt to invest in income-generating opportunities, you can accelerate your path to financial independence. But by avoiding bad debt and managing your borrowing carefully, you ensure that debt works for you, not against you.

Dad was always clear on this: *"Debt can either be a ladder or a trap. It's up to you to decide how to use it."*

⌘⌘⌘

Smart debt management is a critical part of achieving financial freedom. By understanding the difference between good debt and bad debt, you can make informed decisions that help you build wealth, rather than drain your resources. Remember, debt is a tool—one that, when used wisely, can help you reach your financial goals faster.

In the next chapter, we'll explore another key part of Dad's financial philosophy: the importance of living frugally without sacrificing the quality of life. We'll dive into how being smart about spending can give you the freedom to enjoy life today while still securing your future.

Chapter 8

Rule 8: The Power of Frugality Without Sacrificing Quality of Life

One of Dad's most valuable lessons was about finding balance: living well without overspending. He wasn't one to deny himself or our family life's simple pleasures, but he also wasn't interested in keeping up with the Joneses. For Dad, frugality wasn't about deprivation—it was about **intentionality**. It was about spending wisely on what mattered most and avoiding the trap of buying things to impress others or fill a void.

"Frugality gives you freedom," Dad used to say. And he was right. Frugality wasn't about hoarding money or denying yourself the things you enjoy—it was about making sure that every dollar you spent was aligned with your values and goals. It was about making thoughtful decisions that allowed him to enjoy life without sacrificing his future security.

Frugality Isn't About Sacrifice, It's About Choice

The word "frugality" often gets a bad reputation. It conjures images of cutting coupons, living in austerity, or constantly saying no to things you enjoy. But that's not what Dad taught me. His approach to frugality wasn't about self-denial—it was about **making better choices** with your money. It was about making sure that your spending reflected your priorities and helped you build the future you wanted.

For Dad, frugality was a tool that gave him more options. By spending less on things that didn't matter, he had more to invest in things that did—like family experiences, long-term financial security, and the freedom to retire comfortably. His approach was to live below his means, but never in a way that felt like he was sacrificing what was important to him.

I remember one of the key lessons Dad taught me when I got my first paycheck. I was excited, ready to spend it on something fun. But Dad sat me down and said, *"Before you buy anything, ask yourself—does this bring value to your life? Is this making you happier, healthier, or more secure?"* That question changed my perspective on spending forever. It wasn't about avoiding spending money, it was about **spending wisely**.

The Difference Between Being Cheap and Being Frugal

One of the misconceptions about frugality is that it's the same as being cheap. But Dad always made a clear distinction between the two. *"Being cheap,"* he would say, *"means cutting corners and sacrificing quality to save a few bucks. Being frugal means being smart about your spending and getting the most value for your money."*

Here's how Dad explained the difference:

- **Being Cheap**: This is about spending the least amount of money possible, even if it means buying low-quality items that won't last or cutting corners that could cost you more in the long run. For example, buying the cheapest shoes possible only to have them wear out after a few months, forcing you to buy another pair.

- **Being Frugal**: This is about finding ways to save money without sacrificing quality or the things that truly matter to you. It's about making sure that every dollar you spend adds value to your life. For example, buying a high-quality pair of shoes that will last for years, even if they cost more upfront.

Dad believed that **frugality was about value**. It wasn't about denying yourself—it was about making sure that your money was spent on things that brought you long-term value and happiness. He would always ask, *"Will this make my life better today and tomorrow?"* If the answer was yes, it was worth spending on. If not, he'd find a way to save.

Smart Spending Habits That Lead to Financial Freedom

Dad didn't believe in extreme budgeting or cutting out every luxury, but he did have a few smart spending habits that helped him stay frugal while enjoying life. These habits allowed him to save money, avoid unnecessary expenses, and still live comfortably.

Here are some of Dad's most effective strategies:

1. Buy Quality Over Quantity

One of Dad's golden rules was to buy quality, even if it cost a bit more upfront. He believed in investing in things that would last, whether it was clothing, appliances, or even cars. "It's better to buy one good thing that lasts than five cheap things that break down," he would say. This mindset saved him money in the long run because he wasn't constantly replacing items that wore out quickly.

2. Limit Impulse Purchases

One of the easiest ways to blow your budget is through impulse purchases. Whether it's adding extra items to your cart while grocery shopping or buying something online because it's on sale, these small purchases add up. Dad always made it a point to avoid impulse buying. Instead, he would give himself time to think before making any non-essential purchase. If he still wanted it after a few days or weeks, he'd buy it. If not, he saved that money for something else.

3. **Negotiate or Shop Around for Big Purchases**

Another habit Dad had was to always shop around or negotiate on big-ticket items. Whether it was a home repair, a car, or even insurance, he made sure to get multiple quotes and look for deals before making a final decision. *"The first offer is rarely the best,"* he'd say. This habit of comparison shopping saved him thousands of dollars over the years.

4. **Prioritize Experiences Over Stuff**

Dad didn't spend much on fancy clothes, gadgets, or other material things, but he never hesitated to spend on experiences that brought joy to our family. He believed that experiences—like family vacations, special dinners, or outings—brought more happiness and long-term value than physical items. This helped him strike a balance between enjoying life and saving for the future.

5. **Budget, But Keep It Flexible**

Dad believed in budgeting, but he wasn't rigid about it. He saw a budget as a tool to help him stay mindful of his spending, not as a strict set of rules that made life miserable. He'd track his expenses, set savings goals, and allocate money for the things he enjoyed. But he also allowed room for flexibility. If something important came up, like a family event or an unexpected opportunity, he wouldn't hesitate to adjust his budget to make room for it. His motto was *"Save where you can, spend where it matters."*

Avoiding Lifestyle Inflation

One of the biggest challenges people face as their income grows is **lifestyle inflation**. It's the tendency to spend more as you earn more. As your salary increases, so do your expenses—whether it's upgrading to a bigger house, buying a new car, or splurging on luxuries. Dad was always wary of lifestyle inflation, warning me that *"more money doesn't mean you should spend more."*

Instead of letting his lifestyle expand with every raise or windfall, Dad kept his expenses relatively stable. He would allow himself small upgrades or rewards when he hit financial goals, but he didn't drastically change his standard of living. This helped him save more and invest in assets that grew his wealth over time.

For example, when Dad got a promotion, he didn't immediately buy a new car or move to a bigger house. Instead, he would invest the extra income into his savings, stock portfolio, or real estate. His philosophy was that **extra income should be used to build wealth**, not inflate your lifestyle.

This mindset helped him achieve financial independence much faster than if he had increased his spending with every pay raise. He didn't deprive himself, but he also didn't feel the need to keep up with others who were constantly upgrading their lifestyles. Dad found contentment in living well below his means and focused on the things that truly mattered.

The Freedom That Comes With Frugality

For Dad, frugality wasn't about counting every penny or living with less—it was about creating more **freedom**. By making smart financial decisions, he was able to save more, invest more, and ultimately have more freedom in his life. He could retire earlier, take time off when he needed it, and live without the constant stress of financial pressure.

One of the biggest advantages of frugality is that it gives you options. When you live below your means, you're not tied to a paycheck or reliant on debt to sustain your lifestyle. You have the freedom to make choices that align with your values—whether that means retiring early, starting a business, or spending more time with family.

Dad's frugality wasn't about scarcity—it was about abundance. By being intentional with his spending, he had more time, more security, and more freedom to live the life he wanted.

Actionable Steps for Living Frugally Without Sacrifice

Assess Your Current Spending

Take a close look at your current spending habits. Are you spending money on things that truly bring you value? Identify areas where you can cut back without feeling deprived. Redirect that money toward savings or investments.

Prioritize Value Over Cost

Shift your mindset from "What's the cheapest option?" to "What gives me the most value for my money?" Focus on buying quality items that will last, and avoid spending on things that don't add long-term value to your life.

Avoid Lifestyle Inflation

As your income grows, be mindful of lifestyle inflation. Instead of upgrading everything as you earn more, maintain your current lifestyle and use the extra income to invest or save for your future goals.

Create a Flexible Budget

Build a budget that allows you to save while also giving yourself room to enjoy life. Track your spending and savings, but don't be afraid to adjust when necessary. Your budget should be a guide, not a restriction. Make room for the things that matter most to you, and remember that flexibility is key to making your financial plan sustainable in the long term.

Delay Big Purchases to Avoid Impulse Spending

Before making a significant purchase, give yourself time to consider whether it's something you really need or if it's just an impulse buy. Use Dad's method of waiting a few days or weeks before deciding. Often, you'll find that the initial desire fades, allowing you to make more thoughtful decisions.

Frugality as a Path to Financial Freedom

Living frugally isn't about denying yourself—it's about making intentional, smart choices that lead to more financial freedom. By focusing on value over cost, avoiding lifestyle inflation, and spending on what truly matters, you can build a life that's both enjoyable and financially secure. Frugality isn't about cutting back on everything—it's about making your money work for you in ways that bring long-term happiness and success.

As Dad always said, *"It's not about how much you have—it's about what you do with it."*

⌘⌘⌘

Frugality, when done right, gives you freedom—freedom to make choices based on what's important to you, rather than being limited by financial constraints. It's about living below your means without sacrificing the quality of life, so you can focus on building long-term security and wealth.

In the next chapter, we'll talk about how to be adaptable in the face of financial changes. Dad always believed that financial independence wasn't just about building wealth, but also about being flexible enough to pivot when life throws you a curveball. Let's explore how to adjust your strategy when the unexpected happens and why adaptability is key to long-term success.

Chapter 9

Rule 9: Be Ready to Pivot: Adapting to Financial Changes

"Life doesn't always go according to plan. But if you're flexible, you'll always find a way through."

This was one of Dad's core beliefs when it came to money and life in general. He understood that while financial independence is built on solid principles—saving, investing, and living below your means—sometimes life throws a curveball that forces you to adjust your plans. The ability to adapt, to pivot when necessary, is what allows you to stay on track, no matter what obstacles come your way.

Dad was no stranger to life's unexpected turns. I remember when the recession hit, and his company downsized. While many people panicked or fell into financial hardship, Dad remained calm. He knew that unexpected events were part of life, and he had built his financial plan with enough flexibility to adjust when things went wrong. He had always saved more than he spent, kept multiple income streams flowing, and avoided unnecessary debt, which gave him the breathing room to pivot without losing ground.

But adaptability isn't just about being prepared for the worst—it's about recognizing opportunities in changing circumstances. Whether it's a shift in the economy, a new career path, or a personal setback, being ready to pivot gives you the power to turn challenges into opportunities.

The Importance of Financial Flexibility

One of the keys to surviving financial shocks is having a plan that's flexible enough to bend without breaking. Dad was always focused on building flexibility into his financial life. He didn't see his financial plan as a rigid set of rules, but as a living, breathing strategy that could be adjusted as needed.

Here's how Dad built financial flexibility into his life:

1. **Living Below Your Means**

   By consistently living below his means, Dad created a cushion that gave him options when things went wrong. If his income dropped or an emergency came up, he didn't have to scramble to make ends meet.

This allowed him to pivot with less stress, knowing he had room in his budget to handle life's surprises.

2. Building an Emergency Fund

An emergency fund is one of the most important tools for maintaining flexibility. Dad always had six months' worth of living expenses saved, which allowed him to handle any financial setbacks without going into debt. This fund was his safety net, ensuring that he could weather the unexpected without derailing his long-term goals.

3. Diversifying Income Streams

As we discussed in a previous chapter, having multiple income streams gives you more flexibility when one stream dries up. Dad's rental properties, side hustles, and investments provided him with income even when his main job was at risk. By not relying on a single paycheck, he had the freedom to pivot into new opportunities when needed.

4. **Avoiding High Levels of Debt**

Debt limits your ability to adapt. The more you owe, the fewer options you have when financial challenges arise. Dad was always careful about taking on debt and made sure that any loans he had could be managed even if his income dropped. This gave him flexibility to pivot without being weighed down by debt payments.

Learning to Pivot When Life Changes

Being able to pivot isn't just about avoiding financial ruin—it's also about recognizing when it's time to change course, even when things are going well. One of Dad's greatest strengths was his ability to adapt to new circumstances, whether it was shifting economic trends, changes in the job market, or opportunities he hadn't anticipated.

Here are some examples of how Dad used the power of the pivot in his own life:

1. Shifting Career Paths

When the economy changed and Dad's industry began to decline, he didn't cling to his old career path out of fear or habit. Instead, he saw it as an opportunity to try something new. He used his skills to transition into a different role that had better long-term prospects. He didn't wait for the downturn to force him out—he saw the writing on the wall and made the pivot before things got worse.

2. Adapting Investments

Dad was always mindful of changing economic conditions, and he wasn't afraid to adjust his investments when necessary. He never tried to time the market, but he would rebalance his portfolio or shift into more stable assets if the market became volatile. When opportunities arose in real estate or new business ventures, he wasn't afraid to pull out of less profitable investments to take advantage of them.

3. **Personal Setbacks**

Life isn't just about financial changes—sometimes personal setbacks force us to pivot. Whether it was health issues, family challenges, or personal loss, Dad always approached these moments with a mindset of adaptability. He knew that setbacks were inevitable, but how you respond to them defines your ability to move forward. Financial flexibility allowed him to take time off when needed, cover unexpected expenses, and focus on recovery without the added stress of financial strain.

Knowing When to Pivot: Signs It's Time for a Change

One of the hardest things to do is recognize when it's time to pivot. Often, people stick to their financial plans, jobs, or investments even when the signs are pointing toward change. But Dad always believed that being proactive was better than being reactive. He would constantly evaluate his situation and ask himself, *"Is this still working for me?"* If the answer was no, he wasn't afraid to make adjustments.

Here are some signs Dad taught me to look out for:

1. **Job or Industry Instability**

    If your job or industry is showing signs of decline—whether due to technological changes, market shifts, or economic downturns—it might be time to explore new career options. This doesn't mean quitting on a whim, but it does mean preparing yourself for a potential pivot by upgrading your skills, networking in new fields, or starting a side hustle that could turn into a full-time opportunity.

2. **Investment Performance Decline**

    If one of your investments is consistently underperforming and showing no signs of recovery, it might be time to rebalance your portfolio. Sticking with a poor investment out of loyalty or fear of loss can prevent you from seizing better opportunities elsewhere.

Dad believed in giving investments time to grow, but he also knew when to cut his losses.

3. **Personal or Family Changes**

Life events—such as the birth of a child, illness, or family challenges—can often require a shift in your financial priorities. When these events happen, it's important to reassess your budget, savings, and goals. Dad would often adjust his plans when personal circumstances changed, knowing that flexibility was key to maintaining both financial and emotional well-being.

The Power of Resilience and Adaptability

If there's one thing Dad instilled in me, it was the importance of resilience. Life is unpredictable, and even the best financial plans can be upended by things beyond your control. But Dad believed that as long as you were adaptable, you could weather any storm.

Resilience isn't about avoiding challenges—it's about bouncing back from them. Whether it's a job loss, a market crash, or a personal setback, resilience gives you the strength to pivot, adjust your plans, and keep moving forward. It's about knowing that even if one door closes, another one will eventually open.

This mindset of adaptability and resilience is crucial to financial independence. You can't control everything that happens, but you can control how you respond. By being flexible and open to change, you're better equipped to handle whatever life throws your way.

Actionable Steps for Building Financial Adaptability

Keep Your Budget Flexible

Build a budget that allows for adjustments when life changes. This means leaving some wiggle room in your expenses and avoiding rigid rules that don't allow you to adapt. A flexible budget gives you the freedom to handle unexpected expenses or changes in income without falling behind.

Continuously Reevaluate Your Investments

Don't let your investment portfolio sit stagnant. Regularly review your investments and make adjustments as needed. If certain assets are underperforming or no longer align with your goals, don't hesitate to rebalance your portfolio.

Upgrade Your Skills

One of the best ways to remain adaptable in a changing job market is to continuously upgrade your skills. Whether it's through formal education, online courses, or learning on the job, staying ahead of the curve ensures that you're always ready to pivot into new opportunities.

Prepare for the Unexpected

Expect the unexpected. Whether it's job loss, a health emergency, or a major life change, having an emergency fund and a flexible financial plan allows you to handle these events without major disruption. Prepare for the worst, but keep moving toward the best.

Embrace Change

Don't fear change—embrace it. Life is full of unexpected twists and turns, but with the right mindset, you can see these moments as opportunities rather than setbacks. By staying adaptable, you ensure that no matter what happens, you'll find a way to keep moving forward.

⌘⌘⌘

Financial independence isn't about having a perfect plan—it's about being able to adapt when life doesn't go as expected. Dad's rule about pivoting and being flexible was one of the most important lessons he taught me. By building resilience, staying open to change, and knowing when to adjust your course, you can maintain financial security and continue to grow, no matter what life throws your way.

In the next and final chapter, we'll talk about the importance of leaving a legacy. Financial independence isn't just about what you achieve for yourself—it's also about how you set up the next generation for success. Let's dive into how to create a financial legacy that lasts.

CHAPTER 10

RULE 10: LEAVE A LEGACY: BUILDING WEALTH THAT LASTS BEYOND YOU

"True wealth isn't just what you accumulate—it's what you pass on."

Dad used to say this often, and it took me a while to fully understand the depth of his words. Financial independence isn't just about achieving wealth for yourself. It's about ensuring that the security, freedom, and lessons you've gained can be passed on to the next generation. A true legacy isn't built solely on money—it's built on the wisdom and habits that help that wealth endure.

For Dad, creating a legacy was about more than just leaving behind an inheritance. It was about teaching me and my siblings the principles that had allowed him to build financial security so that we could carry those values forward. He didn't want us to simply inherit money—he wanted us to inherit **knowledge**, the same wisdom that had given him the freedom to live life on his own terms.

Leaving a legacy is about ensuring that the benefits of financial independence extend beyond your own lifetime. It's about creating something that lasts—whether it's wealth, a business, or a set of values that your family can rely on for generations.

What It Means to Leave a Financial Legacy

Leaving a financial legacy isn't just about wealth—it's about how that wealth is built, managed, and passed down. Many people think that leaving behind a sum of money is enough, but without the knowledge of how to manage it, that money can quickly be lost. Dad's approach was different. He believed that a financial legacy was twofold: **passing on wealth and passing on financial education.**

Dad always emphasized that the habits, principles, and strategies he used to build wealth were just as important—if not more important—than the money itself. He didn't want us to be dependent on an inheritance. Instead, he wanted to ensure that we had the tools and understanding to create our own financial independence, just as he had.

For Dad, legacy meant:

1. **Leaving Wealth**: Whether through investments, savings, or assets, leaving

behind tangible financial security for the next generation.

2. **Passing on Financial Wisdom**: Teaching the next generation the importance of financial literacy, investing, saving, and living below their means.

By combining these two elements, Dad ensured that his legacy would last—not just as a dollar amount, but as a set of principles that would help us carry forward what he had built.

How to Build a Legacy That Lasts

Building a financial legacy takes careful planning, intentional decision-making, and a focus on the long term. Here are the key elements of creating a legacy that lasts:

1. Teach Financial Literacy

One of the most important things Dad did was teach me and my siblings about money from a young age. He didn't wait until we were adults to talk about budgeting, saving, or investing—he made it a part of our everyday lives. This early education laid the foundation for us to understand the value of money, how to manage it, and how to grow it.

Teaching financial literacy is one of the greatest gifts you can give to the next generation. Whether it's through open conversations, formal education, or setting an example through your own financial habits, passing on knowledge is crucial. Make it a priority to educate your children or loved ones about the basics of money management—budgeting, saving, investing, and the dangers of debt.

2. **Estate Planning: Protecting What You Leave Behind**

Building a legacy isn't just about amassing wealth—it's also about protecting that wealth for the future. Estate planning is an essential part of ensuring that your assets are passed down efficiently and in a way that aligns with your wishes. Dad was diligent about having an estate plan in place to make sure his assets were distributed properly and without unnecessary legal battles.

An estate plan typically includes:

- o **A Will**: Outlining how you want your assets distributed after your passing.

- o **Trusts**: Legal arrangements that hold assets for beneficiaries, offering tax benefits and protecting assets from creditors.

- o **Power of Attorney**: Designating someone to manage your financial affairs if you're unable to do so.

- o **Healthcare Directive**: Outlining your wishes for medical care if you're unable to make decisions.

Estate planning not only protects your wealth but also makes the transition smoother for your family. Without a clear plan, your assets could be tied up in probate or subject to disputes. Dad always said, *"If you've worked hard to build it, make sure it goes where you want it to."*

3. **Create Passive Income Streams for Future Generations**

One of the most powerful ways to leave a financial legacy is by creating assets that continue to generate income long after you're gone. This might include rental properties, dividend-paying stocks, or a family business. These assets can provide your family with a steady stream of income that grows over time, ensuring that the wealth you've built continues to benefit future generations.

Dad's rental properties, for example, became a cornerstone of his legacy. Long after his passing, those properties continued to generate rental income for our family. By investing in assets that appreciate and provide income, you can create a lasting legacy that doesn't just end with the inheritance—it keeps working for your family long after you're gone.

4. **Teach the Value of Hard Work and Responsibility**

While financial education is critical, Dad also believed in passing down the values of hard work, discipline, and responsibility. He never wanted us to rely on his wealth without understanding the effort it took to build it. *"I'm giving you the tools,"* he would say, *"but you have to build with them."*

Teaching the next generation the value of hard work ensures that they don't become complacent or reliant on an inheritance. It encourages them to take ownership of their financial future and to continue building on the legacy you've created. Whether it's through encouraging entrepreneurship, rewarding responsible behavior, or simply setting an example through your own actions, passing on these values helps ensure that your legacy isn't just financial—it's a mindset.

Avoiding Common Pitfalls in Legacy Planning

While building a legacy can be a powerful way to ensure your family's financial future, there are common pitfalls that can undermine your efforts. Here's how to avoid them:

1. **Not Communicating Your Plan**

   One of the most common mistakes is failing to communicate your financial plans and wishes to your family. This can lead to confusion, disputes, and even resentment after your passing. Make sure to have open conversations with your family about your estate plan, your values, and your expectations. Transparency helps prevent misunderstandings and ensures that everyone is on the same page.

2. **Not Having an Estate Plan in Place**

   Without an estate plan, your assets can be tied up in probate, subject to legal fees, or distributed in ways you didn't intend. Make sure to have a legally binding will, and if necessary, trusts in place to ensure that your wealth is passed down smoothly. Work with an attorney or financial planner to create a plan that reflects your wishes and protects your assets.

3. Not Preparing the Next Generation

Leaving a financial inheritance without preparing the next generation to manage it can be a recipe for failure. It's important to pass on the knowledge and skills your family will need to maintain and grow the wealth you've built. Consider involving your children in financial discussions early on and encouraging them to take an active role in managing money.

4. Relying Solely on an Inheritance

While leaving behind financial assets is important, relying solely on an inheritance can create dependency. Encourage your family to continue building wealth on their own, using the tools and values you've passed on. The goal is to create a lasting legacy, not just a one-time windfall.

Creating a Legacy of Values and Wealth

One of Dad's proudest accomplishments wasn't just the wealth he accumulated—it was the legacy of values he passed down. He taught me and my siblings the importance of hard work, frugality, patience, and the ability to adapt. These principles, more than any sum of money, were what gave us the ability to create our own financial independence.

Leaving a legacy isn't just about handing down wealth—it's about handing down the mindset, the habits, and the values that build wealth. Whether it's through financial education, estate planning, or simply setting an example of responsible living, the legacy you leave behind is more than just the money. It's the foundation you've built, the values you've instilled, and the opportunities you've created for the next generation.

Actionable Steps for Leaving a Legacy

Have Open Conversations About Money

Make financial discussions a regular part of family life. Share your experiences, successes, and mistakes with your children or loved ones. By creating a culture of openness around money, you help pass on financial knowledge that lasts.

Create an Estate Plan

Work with a professional to create an estate plan that reflects your wishes. Make sure to include a will, trusts if necessary, and any other legal documents that protect your wealth and ensure it's passed down smoothly.

Invest in Income-Generating Assets

Build a portfolio of assets that continue to provide income, even after you're gone. Whether it's real estate, dividend-paying stocks, or a family business, these assets help ensure that your wealth keeps growing for future generations.

Teach Financial Responsibility Early

Involve your children or loved ones in financial decisions early on. Teach them about budgeting, saving, investing, and avoiding debt. The sooner they learn these principles, the better prepared they'll be to manage their own finances and continue building on your legacy.

⌘⌘⌘

Leaving a legacy is about more than just what you accumulate during your lifetime. It's about passing on the values, habits, and knowledge that helped you achieve financial independence. The wealth you leave behind will be far more impactful if it's accompanied by the understanding of how to manage and grow it.

Dad's legacy wasn't just the financial security he built—it was the mindset he instilled in me and my siblings. His wisdom, discipline, and ability to adapt taught us how to approach life with financial confidence. And that, more than anything, is what has allowed his legacy to endure.

As you work toward your own financial independence, keep in mind that you have the opportunity to build something that lasts beyond your lifetime. By focusing not only on what you leave behind but also on the values and education you pass down, you can create a legacy that empowers future generations to achieve their own success.

Remember: A legacy isn't just about leaving money—it's about leaving a blueprint for how to live a life of financial freedom and independence.

Conclusion: The Journey to Financial Independence

Throughout this book, we've explored the core principles that Dad lived by—rules that guided him to financial independence and gave him the freedom to live life on his terms. These rules weren't complicated, but they were powerful because of their simplicity and consistency.

Here's a quick recap of Dad's ten rules for financial independence:

- **Understand Money and Its True Purpose**: Money is a tool that gives you choices, not the end goal.

- **Save, But Don't Just Save**: Build your financial base by saving with purpose and using your money to grow.

- **Invest in Yourself First**: Your skills, knowledge, and health are your greatest assets.

- **Distinguish Between Assets and Liabilities**: Acquire assets that generate wealth and minimize liabilities that drain it.

- **Create Multiple Income Streams**: Diversify your income to protect against risk and build long-term wealth.

- **Play the Long Game**: Patience and time are your greatest allies in building sustainable wealth.

- **Use Debt Wisely**: Debt can be a tool or a trap—it's all about how you use it.

- **Embrace Frugality**: Living below your means gives you freedom and options without sacrificing quality of life.

- **Be Ready to Pivot**: Life changes, and your ability to adapt is crucial to staying financially secure.

- **Leave a Legacy**: True wealth is not just about what you accumulate—it's about passing on wisdom and opportunity to future generations.

These rules form the foundation of financial independence. They don't promise quick riches, but they do offer something far more valuable: the freedom to live life on your own terms, without being controlled by financial worries or external pressures.

As you apply these rules to your own life, remember that financial independence isn't a destination—it's a journey. It's about making smart, consistent choices that align with your values and long-term goals. It's about creating a life where you have control over your time, your money, and your future.

Whether you're just starting out or already on your way, take these lessons to heart. Follow Dad's rules, adjust them to fit your own circumstances, and never stop learning. The path to financial freedom is within your reach, and with the right mindset and discipline, you can achieve it.

Thank You for Reading

I want to take a moment to thank you for reading this book and joining me on this journey. My hope is that Dad's wisdom, passed down through these pages, will help you find your own path to financial independence. Remember, the lessons in this book are not just for you—they're for the generations that come after you as well. Use them to build a life of freedom, security, and purpose.

Now it's your turn to create your own legacy.